SHAKEN IN THE NIGHT

A SURVIVOR'S STORY FROM THE YELLOWSTONE EARTHQUAKE OF 1959.

ANITA PAINTER THON

To the US Geological Survey Photographic Library, I thank you
for letting me share your pictures.
To the US Forest service, I am grateful that I was able to use
your pictures of my parents.

ISBN: 1499607679
ISBN-13: 9781499607673
Library of Congress Control Number: 2014910569
CreateSpace, North Charleston South Carolina

DEDICATION AND FOREWORD

What is this thing that men call death?
This quiet passing in the night?
'Tis not the end but genesis
Of better worlds and greater light

To my mother who was taken too soon.
I have missed you in my life.

For my sisters Anne and Carole who shared
that fateful night with me.
I love you both!

ACKNOWLEDGEMENTS

To my husband Steve, thank you
for your hours of help, love and support.
To Logan Mickel, you were so kind to give your help,
advice and encouragement. Thanks for editing my book.
To Joanne Girvin, Joanne thank you for all you do to keep the
memory alive of the victims and survivors. You have created
a beautiful visitor center there in West Yellowstone.
I can feel the presence of those people who passed
that night, when I come through the doors.

CONTENTS

AUGUST 17, 1959

At 11:37 pm, the strongest earthquake ever recorded in North America struck the Madison River Canyon in Southwestern Montana. This caused the largest recorded earthquake-landslide in North America.

The quake registered around 7.5 magnitude and caused eighty million tons of rock, earth and debris to roar down Madison Canyon's north wall. It smothered the valley and surged up over 300 feet high and a half mile wide. Along the fault line the land dropped as much as 20 feet. The quake tilted the bed of Hebgen Lake, sending tidal waves over the dam down the canyon to campers six miles away. The waves continued to surge back and forth for at least twelve hours. The landslide traveled at 100 miles per hour burying an area west of the Forest Service's Rock Creek Campground. The slide blocked the course of the Madison River below

Hebgen Dam within minutes. It created a natural dam that backed up the water to form the Earthquake Lake. That lake filled within three weeks, at a depth of 190 feet and 6 miles long. The earthquake trapped hundreds of people, many of whom were injured, some critically, with others later dying in the hospital from their injuries. The majority of the victims, 19 people in all, were buried under the slide. The total loss of life was 28 people.

Rock Creek slide and Earthquake Lake.

READY, SET, GO

My name is Anita Painter Thon. I was at the campground when the earthquake happened. This is the story of my family: my parents, Ray and Myrtle Painter hailing from Ogden, Utah; their older daughter Carole, age 16 at the time of the quake; and twin daughters Anne and myself, age 12.

Summer was winding down and our family had planned a vacation to celebrate our birthdays. We had just turned 12 years old on August 7th. Our older brother Kenneth was in the Army, stationed in California, at Fort Ord. Our family discussed where we should go for our vacation that year. We always took a nice vacation somewhere in the Western United States, Canada, or British Columbia, usually an area where Dad could to a little fishing. My mother wanted to go to California this year to visit my brother in California.

He had gotten really sick on maneuvers months before and I think she wanted to check on him, to make sure he was doing better. But Dad wanted to go to Yellowstone Park to show us the sights. Both places sounded really fun to visit, but the deciding factor was our Labrador, Princess. She was a black Labrador with lots of personality. She loved to go in the car everywhere we went and we loved the idea of taking her along with us. We could leave her in the trailer or campground where it was cool if we left to go fishing or hiking. We were really excited about going because we had a brand new 25 foot trailer to stay in. It was so nice with two bedroom areas, a hammock, and kitchen area with stove, oven, refrigerator and nice bathroom with a shower. It wasn't like roughing it at all! My Dad loved to fish, that is the main reason they had bought the trailer for fishing trips like this. My parents used to go to Yellowstone when they were first married. They usually took our older brother Ken when he was a little boy, but this was the first trip for the girls. My Dad loved Yellowstone and West Yellowstone and knew the area well. He couldn't wait to share this experience with us.

Our family had prepared well before the trip. We knew we would be gone for a couple of weeks and we would be getting home just before school started. So we went clothes shopping, preparing everything for school so we wouldn't be rushed to do it when we got home from our vacation. My Mother was obsessed with cleanliness. She kept telling us that if anything happened to our family on this trip, we wouldn't want family members to come into a messy house. Believe me our house was never messy because Mom was a clean freak. So we had a big cleaning party to please her, cleaning out closets and drawers. She seemed to be worried about our safety. It was like she was having a premonition of something bad happening to our family in Yellowstone. She checked into whether the life and property insurance was in order. It made us uncomfortable when she would talk like that, so we would tell her to stop worrying. We would ease her fears by telling her everything was going to be fine, it's going to be a great trip.

From what I can remember our drive to Montana was really fun. We were so happy to be together. Mom and Dad worked full time, and so we didn't see them as much as we would like to. Usually we would head to Pine View Dam near Ogden, where we would spend the weekend, fishing and hiking and things like that. So this vacation was something we really looked forward to. We would be having lots of quality time with our parents. The weather was beautiful; August is a good time for a trip because it isn't as hot as the beginning of the summer.

We were having such a great time singing, telling stories and feeding the bear cookies. The bear was Dad. We were kidding with him because back in 1959 the bears would approach the cars for food. You could actually feed them from the car. It sounds exciting, but it created a big problem in Yellowstone and the surrounding areas. The bears were starting to be a real nuisance, raiding campgrounds all over the place. It kind of scared me when I thought the bears could be where we were going. We had gone camping once in the mountains, where we had slept in our car for the night. The next morning we saw paw prints on the car windows.

Bear paws we thought! While we weren't certain it had been a bear, we were panicked just the same. That has always kind of freaked me out. I kept thinking it was good thing I was in a car not a tent.

We spent a couple of days in Yellowstone Park driving and hiking and seeing the waterfalls and the different sights. We saw lots of animals roaming around, including bears. We took many pictures and went through film like crazy. We loved seeing Old Faithful Geyser and the Old Faithful Lodge which was really quaint looking inside and out. I thought how fun it would be to stay there sometime, if we ever get the chance to come back again. We went into a rock shop in Yellowstone. They had the most beautiful rocks with mineral deposits on them. All of us girls got jewelry of some kind made from the rocks. At the park we wandered around looking at the different sights with the steam vents, bubbling mineral pools, hot mud pots and geysers. The pools were really pretty, very colorful, turquoise blue, green, orange and other colors. I had read in a book about the bison, how they die suddenly from some of the vapors or gases that come up while they were grazing, so I didn't know how safe it was to be around all those fumes. Anyway it smelled really bad like rotten eggs. That is what I remember most about it.

Vacationers were allowed to walk out along the board walk to look at the pools and mud pots. We had heard stories about people accidently falling into some of those pools and being killed. I wasn't sure if those stories were true or not, but it made you feel uneasy being around them. I could see how someone could accidently fall in because a lot of areas didn't have railings to hold on to. What I remember is how uneasy my mom seemed to be. She didn't seem to be enjoying herself at all. She always had a worried look on her face. She kept saying with the geysers, hot mud pots, bubbling mineral pools and steam vents it seems like the ground is alive, the area can't be safe. She said" I wonder if they have lots of earthquakes here?" It was in the early afternoon when were about to leave Yellowstone Park for West Yellowstone when she said," Let's get out of here before the whole place blows up". So weird she would say that because her worst fears were about to come true!

IT'S A BEAUTIFUL DAY

On the afternoon of Monday, August 17th we were on the road to West Yellowstone. It was still such a beautiful afternoon with the sun shining. Mom seemed to be much happier and enjoying herself, now that we were away from the park and from the ground that was alive! Dad was in hurry mode. He was on a mission to get to West Yellowstone as fast as possible. He wanted to find a nice place in the campground where we were headed. Dad talked about where we would be staying and how beautiful the camping area was. He told us about people he knew from Utah that had vacationed in this area. They said the fishing was great and they especially loved the scenery. It was a very popular place to camp for vacationers and the camp sites usually fill up fast. Having a trailer to stay in isn't that convenient; a lot of campgrounds don't have hook ups for trailers and space large enough to park a trailer. Because of those limitations, my Dad chose this area.

I remember driving past Hebgen Dam. We saw boats and people fishing off the banks. Our drive down the Madison River Canyon was so beautiful with the cliffs, ridges and mountains and the Madison River. I remember looking out and taking in all the terrain and thinking Dad is right, it is a beautiful area. We drove the six miles down the canyon, passing some quaint little cafes and motels where you could eat and stay, with decks and patios that backed up to the river. They looked so inviting. I thought someday that I would like to come back there and stay, or at least stop and see everything. We asked Dad if we could stop for a little look, but he said we were pressed for time.

When we finally arrived at our destination most of the campers had left or were leaving for home already because it was the end of a weekend. Even though it looked somewhat crowded, we were able to find a nice spot by the road. Today, I still can picture in my mind the first place we had stopped to park the trailer. It had some shade, but lots of sun which I liked. Sometimes it can be too shady and cold at the campground, especially when you are in the mountains. We all thought we had the perfect spot picked out, but not my Dad. He took a little walk and came back to announce that he had found even a better place to park the trailer. We weren't really happy about moving to a different location, because we had already started to unload coolers and things. We knew Dad was serious about changing camps though, so we had to pack up everything and move as he had requested. He told us he had found this nice spot that was more private, near the Madison River in a grove of pine trees backed up to the mountains.

After the move we all agreed it was a much better site, with more shade if we had to leave Princess in camp. The campground started to fill up fast as it approached late afternoon. We got the camp set up with chairs and prepared the site for a bon fire we would be having later in the evening. We wanted to cook hot dogs on a stick and of course Marshmallows for S'mores. This was what we kids had planned, whether Mom and Dad would go along with this idea we would see. A lot of the campers had to pitch their tents near the river I noticed. I believe there was a group of scouts that came late, so they just laid out the sleeping bags on the bank of the river.

Unfortunately that move from the original spot for us turned out to be a grave mistake for our family, as we would find out later that night. Why, why, did we move?

The Rock Creek campground, from what I can remember, was in a loop or circle that backed up to the mountains. The river was adjacent to our camp. I remember it was late afternoon; the sun was shining, but starting to set. It was nice and warm for being in the mountains. I could see lots of bugs in the air, but not mosquitoes. The area we were staying in looked so green and lush for that time of year. I loved the smell and the sound of the river, campfires burning, and the aroma of dinner being cooked on open fires. I could see lots of camping sites which were tents, trailers, or just sleeping bags stretched out on the ground. I remember thinking to me, there is no way you would get me sleeping out in just a sleeping bag on the ground. That would be too scary with all the critters that roam around this place.

On our afternoon walk, we stopped and talked to a lot of nice friendly campers. My Dad wanted to get a current fishing report for the morning; he was able to talk to a guy who had just returned from fishing and even showed us his catch for the day. That made my Dad so excited, he couldn't wait until morning. As we walked on, we waved and said hello to people we passed. We were greeted by a Forest Ranger who wanted to update us on bear sightings and how they'd been raiding campsites. He said the bears were aggressive when looking for food and not shy about getting it anyway they could. They were getting into coolers, tents, and food storage containers. He explained that it would be a really good idea for everyone to keep their campsites clean of any food items. He told us not to leave anything out that could possibly draw the bears in. The bears were even getting on the top of trailers rocking them. I wasn't too worried though. I thought we were safe in our trailer, as the bears couldn't open the door to get inside.

We later headed back to our camp after a short stop to look at the Madison River. We started our great fire for the evening and prepared a really good steak dinner with fried potatoes—saving the hotdogs and marshmallows for later—cooked on a grill over the open flame. It was the most beautiful night with a huge full moon that shone down on the whole camp into the meadow and the ridges and mountains. It illuminated everything, as though we had lanterns hanging in the trees. You could see the mountain range really well. We had a nice evening together talking, laughing and planning our fishing trip in the morning. We were all getting very tired after a long day of driving, but knew we needed to make our camp bear-proof so everything was cleaned up and secured away.

Just as we had days before, we were deciding who would be sleeping where for the night. My sister Carole always chose the back seat of our car. For some reason she didn't like sleeping in the trailer. I remember well, I got on this kick about wanting to sleep in the hammock bed, which was over the top of my parent's bed in the back of the trailer. I wanted to sleep there but my Mom said "no not tonight," even though I begged her she wouldn't give in. She said that I needed to sleep in the bed in the front area of the trailer with Anne. I got really upset with my Mom and I wouldn't talk to her. I'm so sorry now that I got mad at her. I would regret that part of the evening forever. I would also find out later that her decision for me not to sleep there would later save my life. Did she sense something?

TERROR IN THE NIGHT

We had just settled into our beds. I fell asleep really fast, but then something woke me up. I felt like I was half asleep, or that I was dreaming that the trailer was rocking or swaying. I remember being so annoyed! I just wanted to sleep but I couldn't because of the rolling or swaying of the trailer. I called out to Dad, "Dad make Princess lay down, she is rocking the trailer." He never answered me back; I thought that was odd, but then I thought he was asleep and maybe couldn't hear me.

I really woke up when I heard the strangest noise outside. It was a scary sound I had never heard before, or ever wanted to hear again. It was a deafening roar of wind, or the sound of a huge locomotive train with many engines, far off in the distance. I remember lying there trying to think if I had seen any trains, or train tracks on our drive down the canyon, but

I hadn't. I kept thinking how could a train be coming into our campground? The roaring sound was getting unbelievably louder and closer, like it was headed straight for our trailer. Whatever was coming was huge, I thought! I remember that my heart was pounding so hard, like it was coming out of my chest. I was breathing faster and faster because I was so scared. I wanted to scream as loud as I could, because I didn't know what was happening. I remained in my bed, so did Anne. She was awake too, but we never spoke to each other, not one word. She looked at me, as terrified as I was. It seems like we were prompted not to try and get up; we talked about this later in our lives and we both felt we were being protected, or held there by angels. It was like there was a glass bubble over us, and they were keeping us from leaving the safety of our bed. I can't imagine if we would have tried to get up and go outside of the trailer, we would have surely been killed.

Suddenly, we were hit really hard by something. It was like we had been in the worst automobile accident you could ever experience. The trailer exploded apart, rolling several times. As it was happening I remember seeing things flying through the air like glass, cupboards, and clothes. I was praying for it to stop and that we wouldn't be killed. The trailer rocked and rolled, eventually cracking open like an egg, letting in the moon light. As this was happening, Anne and I pulled the quilts over our heads and screamed and cried for our parents' help.

Then it was over. The roar was gone, replaced with the sound of water, both dripping inside the ravaged trailer and water running outside. We were in shock but relieved that we were still alive. We could hear people moaning, screaming and crying for help. My sister Anne and I just fell out of the trailer into water that was chest high. It smelled of dirt and gasoline mixed together and there was debris in it. I was stunned at what I saw; it looked like we were in the river. I looked around; searching for the train that I thought had hit our trailer. I was as confused as to what had happened. The only thing I saw was dark cold water everywhere. Suddenly the realization hit me: we were in the Madison River!

Anne and I cried and screamed for our family. What I didn't know until later was that what had hit us wasn't a train, but a wall of water from the 20 foot-high tidal wave from the Hebgen Dam above us. The roaring, deafening sound we heard was the sound of the mountain sliding down and up the other side of the canyon, which had caused hurricane-force winds. The slide from the mountain had blocked the flow of the Madison River and our campground was quickly filling up with water. It was a nightmare comes true!

It was sheer terror not knowing what was happening and not being able to find our family. I was so glad I at least had Anne with me. I remember seeing a lady sitting on a large boulder that had come down from the slide. She had a white robe on and was smoking a cigarette. She casually said to us "You'll be okay, don't worry, and stop your crying." I remember looking at her and thinking she was crazy. We can't find our family, the water is rising and we don't know what to do next. She must have been in shock as well.

Anne and I went back to the trailer to search for our parents. We thought they must be trapped inside the trailer, because the back of it was smashed down from the tidal wave and pine trees that had fallen. We swam around to the back of the trailer where there was a huge gaping hole. We took turns diving under the really cold water, reaching to see if we could feel their heads without getting cut from the twisted torn metal. We didn't know whether they were still in the trailer and trapped in their bed. I'm not sure how many times we dove under the water feeling for them, but we were freezing cold. At the same time we were hysterically crying from fear. Anne and I could hear boulders smashing together and the sound of dirt sliding down the mountain. The sound echoed through the whole campground. I did notice that the loop we had walked around that afternoon was gone. It was now replaced with a huge wall of dirt. I don't know if we knew until later what had actually happened that we had been in a horribly strong earthquake, until heard people talking about it later. Anne had been cut from the flying glass and was bleeding from her lip. We had bumps and bruises but we were so blessed not to be seriously injured. We were grateful for that!

Carole would tell me years later that she was asleep in the car when she felt the earthquake happening. She heard that deafening roar and raised her head up to look out. She said the tidal wave hit the car and the force of the water rolled it over, shoving it into a large tree. It smashed her face and head into the door of the car, injuring her. She said she was pinned in the car, but was able to climb out. She noticed us by the trailer, but didn't come over where we were. She was so scared she would drown, so she left. She said we knew how to swim and she thought we would be okay. She had gone off instead to try and find our parents. To our great relief, she did. When Anne and I were at our worst moment, when we were losing hope and thinking we were going to die, Carole called to us from a ridge above our camp to come to her. I really do not know what we would have done had Carole not found us. We would probably have drowned because the water was getting deeper. We couldn't see beyond our situation. It was such a horrible thing to go through, being so young and alone. We were so happy to see Carole; we just hugged and hugged her. She gave us a glimmer of hope that we were going to get out alive.

Carole told us that she had found a silhouette, a person sitting there in the dark. She heard someone say her name. "Carole, come! I need help. I am hurt." It was Mom, sitting on a rock right near where the slide had ended. Carole asked her how she ended up being there. She told her after everyone had gone to bed, she decided to go down to the river to wash her hair around 11:30 pm. Dad didn't even know that she had left the trailer. That is where she was when the earthquake started. The force of the tidal wave and hurricane force-wind smashed her up against the slide, crushing her chest and nearly severing her arm. She was then thrown back out by the slide where she landed. Carole told us that our trailer was probably about 30 to 40 feet where the slide ended; it was a miracle we weren't buried alive.

She had taken ahold of Mom's arm and started walking her up the hill away from the water, where she saw a light from a lantern that was hanging in a tree. This light turned out to belong to a nurse named Mildred Greene. The Greene's and their small son were camped in a tent. They were nearly buried by the slide as well. Carole told Mildred that her Mom was badly injured and bleeding heavily, that she had lost her arm. She had to lean against a tree for support. Mildred immediately took and laid her on a sleeping bag on the ground, where she started working, trying to stop her bleeding. As minutes went by, Mildred told us that we needed to look for more clean dry sheets, or blankets to use for bandages because Mom's arm was bleeding through the bandages due to torn arteries. It was almost severed at the elbow. She also had a compound fracture of that arm and the bone was sticking out into her neck. Her chest was crushed, lung punctured and she was having a hard time breathing. We were able to find a large trunk that held some dry, clean items we could use to change her bandages. As bad as she was, I never heard her cry or complain about her injuries. She looked like she was in a daze; I'm sure she was in shock. Her long dark hair had dirt, twigs and debris in it. Her clothes had been torn off from the wind and tidal wave. Someone had given her a blanket to cover up with. We loved our Mom so much and were so upset and sad that she was injured so badly. We are so thankful that Mildred was there, and that she went to work to stop the bleeding.

Carole eventually found Dad walking up the hill towards where we all were. Dad said when the trailer started swaying he immediately thought it was the bears. He said he went outside to look around and when he stepped off the last step he was tossed up into the air. He realized it was an earthquake, not bears! After the shaking stopped, he said he heard a really loud bang in the canyon. In the next minute or so he saw a 20 foot wall of water coming over the tops of the pine trees. He said that he tried to run back to the trailer, but he knew he would never make it so he grabbed ahold of a pine tree that was uprooted before getting washed away.

Afterwards he recalled Anne and myself screaming and crying for help, but not being able to get to us because he was pinned by a large pine tree about 50 yards away.. He knew he was hurt badly from the tree and had yelled for help, thinking he was going to drown. Eventually three men came to his rescue, but not until his clothes had been torn off by both water and wind.

After being freed, he had started to walk away when the men tried to stop him, claiming he couldn't go until he received medical attention. His response had been "The hell I can't. I got to go find my family."

He told us he had stopped by the trailer to get dry clothes for us and to look for Mom. He didn't have any clothes with him when we saw him. Besides, there wasn't a trailer left for him to find anything. Due to the arteries that had been cut in his leg, he too was bleeding heavily. Mildred and some other people were able to lay him out on the ground to tie a tourniquet to help control it He was in shock like Mom.

EVACUATION

We were so relieved to finally be together. All of us were safe and we were going to get out alive, as a family. Little did we know how bad our parents' injuries really were! Our reunion was short lived, because we were told that some men had driven up to the spill way in a forest service truck to check out if the Hebgen Dam had sustained any major damage due to the quake. They were able to see with flash lights and lanterns that the dam did have some major cracks. They came back in a hurry to report to the people in the campground that we needed to evacuate the area because they were worried about the dam breaking. So we had to hurry out of there and move towards higher ground.

Once more, we were afraid for our lives. Some kind people, who had a trailer that wasn't damaged, offered to put our critically injured parents in their trailer, using it as an ambulance. They needed to be cared for and it was the only way to move them. It turns out their trailer was in the spot that we had originally stopped at the first time. I kept thinking about that. Why did we move and change our camping site? We should have stayed where we were! That thought still haunts me today.

My sisters and I were being cared for by some wonderful people in the camp, who took us under their wing, so to speak. We were placed in a car and driven up Madison Canyon to be near our parents. Everyone was so kind and cared for us so lovingly. We were appreciative and thankful to have them watching over us. We were so young we don't remember the names of any of the people who helped us. They kept telling us several times that we were being so brave, that our parents would be proud of us. I remember thinking to myself that I wasn't sure why they thought we were so brave when actually we were so scared.

We finally reached an area up the canyon, which is now named Refuge Point. It was a high ridge in the canyon which would provide protection for us if the dam should break that night. The ground rumbled all night long--aftershocks I guess. We could see dust in the air and the sound of landslides still happening all around us. You could still hear big boulders crashing down in the canyon. My sisters and I never slept a wink that night. We were too afraid of something happening. It was a beautiful moonlit night during the quake, but it started to sprinkle a light rain that morning. The aftershocks were still happening. The ground would rumble so we didn't know whether it was thunder from a storm or the earth was still moving. Most of the people on the ridge had been awake all night like just like us. Everyone was still running around in pajamas and robes, the three Painter children included. Anne and I had on white flannel pajamas that originally had little tiny blue flowers on them. They were now covered with black dirt, gasoline, and blood. The smell made us sick and we couldn't wait to be able to get cleaned up. Carole had only a coat on without anything under it. She had a huge black eye that covered a big area of one side of her face. She also had an eye injury that would later require surgery to fix.

HELP HAS ARRIVED

As dawn approached, we first heard and then saw a plane fly over. Then all of the sudden the Forest Service smoke jumpers appeared, parachuting to the ridge. We felt we had more angels that had been sent to help us. We were surprised and relieved that they had come and were setting up a rescue operation for the stranded campers. They also were dropping food and water supplies. I remember seeing men and kids running to see what were inside the crates they had dropped. My sisters and I couldn't get excited about anything, because we were so worried about our parents. I remember being envious that the kids seemed to be having fun with their families, and I was just sad. Really sad. The campers had set up an area out in the meadow on this ridge where a breakfast was being prepared with whatever food items they could come up with. My sisters and I never ate; we just wanted to get our parents some help.

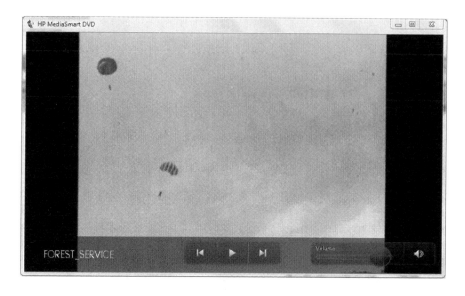

The original Smoke Jumpers landing on the ridge 1959.

SOS

Later on in the early morning we left the main group of campers to head up the canyon with six to eight critically injured people, including our parents, to the Hebgen Dam. This is where we were told to go to await the helicopters that were being sent to transport the injured to West Yellowstone. From there they would be taken to the nearest hospital in Montana for treatment.

We waited. It seemed like a really long time. We later heard that the delay in organizing help was over six hours long. Anne and I were sitting outside the trailer when Dad called for us to come inside the trailer. We started to enter; I almost fainted at the sight. Our parents were lying on a mattress that was completely blood soaked. Mom called out "Please, don't let my daughters see me like this!" and so we were quickly ushered out. Carole was old enough to help with Mom and Dad's care. Carole told us Mom was having hard time breathing on her back because of her punctured lung filling up with fluid. She wanted to lie on her side but the bone from her arm was sticking into her neck. The doctor told the nurse to put gauze in between the bone and her neck so it wasn't sticking her and to keep her on her side.

I remember as we were leaving the trailer dad called out to us "Girls, you have to get help now or your Mother is going to die." This was upsetting; what were we to do? We started crying again and felt like we were on an emotional roller coaster. First we would have a little good news, which would quickly turn to bad news. Anne and I said to each other what are we supposed to do? We have no way of getting help; we are just little girls, only twelve years old. We later got this idea to make an SOS out of something that was white that could be seen from the air. We decided to make a sign on the little service road next to the spill way. Someone had left a canister of pancake flour sitting out. We thought it was perfect and proceeded to make a huge SOS sign. After our efforts, a small plane flew over and tipped its wings at us as if it saw our message. We realized later, that help was already coming; it was just taking a long time. Nevertheless, the experience with the plane gave us hope and relief; we had done as Dad had asked. Later on we saw that someone had placed a much larger SOS in front of the spill way.

Eventually things got moving. Patients were being prepared on stretchers and the pitiful camp was ready for the helicopters. They arrived, touching down on the bank near the dam. The critical patients were going to be transported to the West Yellowstone airport where an airplane had been converted to an air ambulance. Mom and dad were the first to be loaded on the helicopter. I remember standing there on the bank watching them. My thoughts were that it was so neat that they were being flown out of the area. They looked really pale and sick. I kept thinking to myself don't worry they're going to be okay; they will soon be at the Hospital to get the help they needed. We later found that they were taken to a hangar in West Yellowstone and placed on hay bales while preparations were being made to fly them out in the air ambulance.

We heard years later that the wait was long for them. Time was so precious and it seemed like everything was taking so long. Back in 1959 things were really different; the military was used in rescue operations. Today a helicopter would have been sent instantly and the patient flown to big, modern trauma centers. The helicopters we were waiting for were on assignment to Missoula, Montana. They had to go back to their base and refuel, then prepare to fly to Yellowstone. This took a half of a day. My sister Carole says she thinks some helicopters were finally sent from Hill Air Force Base.

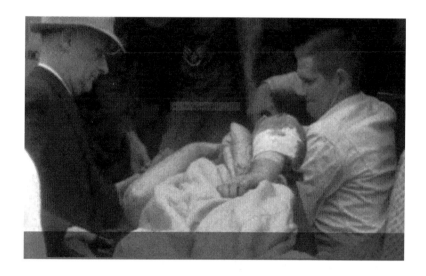

Mom being evacuated.

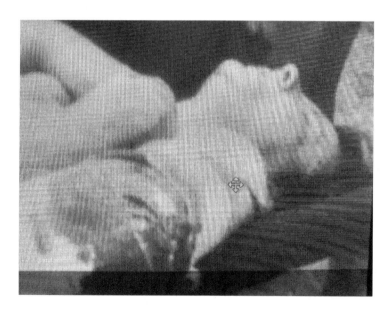

Last time I saw her.

Evacuation helicopter to West Yellowstone.

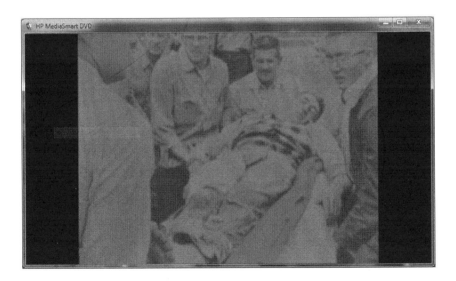

Dad being evacuated.

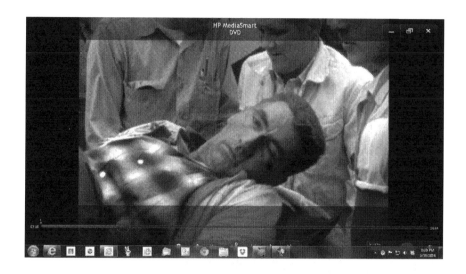

*The next time I saw Dad was days
later in a hospital in Ogden.*

RESCUE

The rescue operation for the rest of us was in process. Rather than fly everyone out, which would be a lot of people, a plan was being made to bulldoze an exit road. A lot of people still had their cars and trailers. Not us. We were leaving a demolished car, trailer and all of our belongings behind. But we were all alive and thankful for that!

We sat in cars and watched and waited as road crews worked throughout the day making a substitute exit road along the steep mountainside parallel to the one that had been damaged by the quake and fallen into Hebgen Dam. Finally, at 6 PM that night, the road was now passable. The cars without trailers went through first. Then the cars pulling trailers were pulled through by the bulldozers. It was a really, really bumpy, dusty ride but we were getting out of there, which made us so happy! We eventually made it to a drivable road.

Eighteen hours after the quake we made it to the Montana State College gym in Bozeman, Montana where a Red Cross center had been set up for evacuees. We learned that our parents were in a hospital in Bozeman. We wanted to go see them, but it wasn't possible to arrange. I remember how wonderful it was to be able to take a shower and wash my hair to get rid of that awful smell. The Red Cross volunteers were so kind and understanding to us. We were given some new jeans and T-shirts to put on. We didn't have any information about how long we would be there, or where we would be going afterwards. We just felt safe and secure at last and so thankful to be there. We were fed a meal and had a comfortable bunk bed to sleep in that night. We were all so exhausted for not sleeping since the earthquake.

I hadn't realized it that night, but we would later find out that horrible earthquake was about to change our lives forever.

Mom with Carole, Anne and Anita.

THE FAMILY

Later that day our aunts, Phyllis and Bessie, came to claim us at the college. We were happy to see family members, but we were whisked away so fast. I wanted to see our parents, but that wasn't possible. Instead we were driven immediately to Aunt Phyllis's house in North Ogden. In later years Mom's Brother Ellis would tell us that he was not happy about us being driven back to Utah so soon. They were hoping to see us; they felt like we should stay in the area to be near our parents. They lived in Black Foot Idaho and wanted to take us there.

I remember everywhere we stopped along our drive back to Utah; my aunts would tell everyone that we had been in the Yellowstone earthquake. I didn't want that attention. I wanted to forget that terrible day, but they kept reminding us by telling everyone about it. Shortly after arriving in Ogden, probably that next day, we were taken to buy us some new clothes because we would be staying with our Aunt Phyllis for a while. We were happy to being staying there because we had a little three year old cousin, Peggy. She helped brighten those gloomy days.

We were in a bedroom putting our clothes away after shopping, and my Aunt Bessie came and sat down on the bed next to us. She said, "I hate to tell you girls this, but your Mom has died from her injuries." We were in shock; I didn't believe her at first. I asked my aunt how she could have died; she only had a cut arm. I didn't cry. My sister Anne and I just bolted out of the house to be alone, to be away from everyone to sort out our feelings.

Mom's funeral was held on August 22nd 1959. She was 42 years old at the time of her death. She had worked as a manager of the bakery at an America Food Store. She was well-liked and loved by her coworkers, family and friends. At her viewing it was so hard to look at her beautiful face, and see the bruising that couldn't be hidden by makeup. It made me realize the pain and suffering she went through before her death. I was angry because I never got to tell her goodbye, or tell her how sorry I was for getting mad at her that night. She saved my life, I will always remember that. It's so important that you live your life with no regrets. Dad was unable to attend Mom's funeral because he was still being treated in an Ogden Hospital for his major injuries. We were still in deep shock and mourning the loss of our beloved Mother. It was hard for us kids to go to the viewing and funeral alone, because everyone wanted to know what happened, all the details. It was making us relive the earthquake again by talking about it. It was so painful and emotional for us that we would start crying over and over again.

Our Brother Ken was flown from Fort Ord, California to be with Mom and Dad in the hospital. He was with Mom when she died. He was only 20 years old at the time and lucky to have been spared the horror of the earthquake. But he was now forced to be the care giver to three younger sisters whether he wanted to or not. Dad was suffering from major depression; he was fighting to want to live without Mom, which made it very stressful for us to deal with. We didn't know what to do to help him get through it. We were trying to heal from the horrible experience we had gone through as well. I guess you could say he had survivor's guilt. We all went through similar feeling: why had our lives been spared, while others had died?

Dad was eventually released to the care of his sister Phyllis, who was a nurse by profession. She had to change his bandages several times a day in addition to watching Anne and I. Carole went to stay with another aunt on Mom's side of the family. When school started we were forced to change schools because it was too hard driving us back and forth every day. We were sad because we missed our friends, house, and especially Mom. Dad never remarried for years and so we were farmed out to different relatives in the summer months. Thankfully about six months later we were able to return back to the home that we loved. Memories of Mom were there, that helped comfort us and gave us the strength to carrying on. During the months we were in school it was just the three girls left at home alone. It wasn't a happy childhood. Our neighbors did what they could to help ease our burdens. Dad did remarry later on in life, but continued to struggle with major depression for years and mentally never got over that night. He died of cancer a day before my son Zach was married in 1986.

Eventually we all grew to adulthood. I'm now married to a wonderful man, Steve. We have two sons, Zachary and Ryan, who are married to wonderful women. They have blessed our lives with seven grandchildren. Anne was married and has two sons and seven grandchildren. Carole never married.

BACK TO YELLOWSTONE

I was able to go back to Yellowstone in the 1990's for the first time since the earthquake. We went with our son Zachary and his wife Danielle. Also, Steve's parents came with us to see the quake area for the first time. It was surreal to see the slide again and to see the tops of the pine trees from the Rock Creek campground sticking out of the water. In the daylight for the first time I could see how the slide from the mountain had come down and gone across the other side of the canyon. The slide is what caused that horrible deafening roar we heard that night. I was looking at the rocks from the slide-about 300 feet deep, from what I understand- and kept thinking about the nineteen victims buried beneath.

Memorial Plaque dedicated to the victims of the earthquake.

I saw the gigantic boulder that was part of the buttress that held the mountain up. It had ridden the slide down like a surf board, landing across the canyon. This is where the names of the 28 victims are memorialized on a bronze plaque. I had a really hard time being there. My thoughts were, like always, how did I get out alive? I was so thankful that my life was spared and I was able to grow up and have a family.

We went inside the visitor center that was located next to the Memorial Boulder. Once inside I saw a huge picture on a wall of my sister Carole with her black eye. We watched a film depicting the quake when it started and the damage it had done, as well as stories about the campers and their experiences. It also mentioned those that were critically injured, killed, or who had later died of their injuries. In the film it showed Mom and Dad being loaded into the helicopter to be transported. It really got me teary eyed because I could remember how bad they were injured. Today I still have little flash backs, nightmares, smells of dirt and gasoline together, and noises that haunt me. People ask me if I remember the earthquake, and my answer is always the same: I will never forget!

In 2009 the survivors of the Yellowstone Earthquake were invited back for the 50th Anniversary. I was excited to go back once again, but also apprehensive of being in the area. This time only my husband Steve and I went back for the 50th Anniversary. My sister Carole has never been back since the earthquake and tells me that she has no desire and is terrified of the thought of being there again. She told me she still has nightmares after all those years. She still pictures Mom and Dad with their injuries in her mind. She was old enough to be in the trailer helping care for them. Anne and I had been spared that.

Anne has never been back either. Her family has been to Quake Lake and the visitor center and have encouraged her to go back, but to date she hasn't gone. I wanted to go again with the promise of seeing and thanking people who may have helped us, or cared for our family during and after the quake. I didn't want to stay in the canyon though. I didn't feel safe sleeping there. I didn't want to be near a large body of water or backed up to a mountain that could fall down on me.

50TH ANNIVERSARY OF THE EARTHQUAKE

The 50th Anniversary program started out with the reen-actment at Refuge Point, the ridge where we were taken for protection the night of the earthquake because of the fear that Hebgen Dam could break. The Forest Service Rangers first of all talked about how the smoke jumpers were sent that early dawn to set up an evacuation center and to help care for the injured. We heard a plane fly over and then came the smoke jumpers. Not the same men of course, but it did bring back a lot of raw memories. I was able to meet three smoke jumpers that helped Mom and Dad. They remembered them well, and told me that as badly as they were injured they were brave and never complained about their injuries. They were also with our parents when they were flown to the West Yellowstone Airport. I hugged all of them and thanked them for helping and told them how thankful we were that they came that early dawn. I was interviewed by some reporters that day and I was able to give an account of the night of the earthquake and the days afterwards.

Later that evening we all met at a hotel in West Yellowstone where they continued with the program. The survivors all mingled together and I was able to meet and speak to people who were camped in other camping grounds around Rock Creek such as the Halford Cabins and Bear Creek, which overlooked the Rock Creek campground. Those survivors told us me that after the earthquake they could hear horrible screams and crying coming from Rock Creek campground. They said what they heard that night was so horrible and still haunts them today. They said they felt so helpless because they couldn't do anything to help us. When they knew I was a survivor of the Rock Creek campground, they said let me give you a belated big hug for what you and your family went through.

Plaque at Refuge point.

Survivors meet at Refuge point for a welcome program and to meet other survivors.

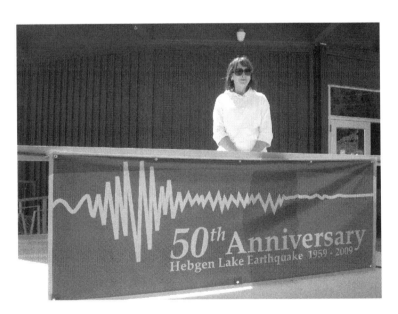

Welcome sign by the Forest Service.
Thank You!.

Reenactment of the Smoke Jumpers at Refuge point.

Meeting the original Smoke Jumpers at the 50th Anniversary.

50th Anniversary program with a picture of the survivors.

I wanted to be able to meet the nurse that cared for our parents. I was told she may not be there as she lived in Billings and is now in her 80's. After an hour or so I learned that she was there and she would be speaking on the program that evening. I couldn't wait to be able to meet her. She spoke about her experience that night, about her family sleeping in a tent and feeling the earthquake happening and opening the flap to see a wall of dirt and water flood inside. Her young son had a fever that night and so he was sleeping close by his parents rather than in the other part of the tent. That fever saved his life because a huge pine tree had smashed through the tent where he would have been.

She spoke about taking care of the victims that included a story about my parents. I got really teary eyed again to hear how kind and loving she was to them when they were hurt so badly. After the program ended I was able to meet other families. One man I met was the Stowe family's son who had lost both parents in the earthquake. His Mom's body had never been recovered; she is still buried under the slide. I told him how sorry I was for his loss. He told me that he was only three years old when it happened and he doesn't really remember a lot about his parents. He wasn't with them on their trip to Yellowstone; he stayed home with his grandparents while his parents went on a fishing trip. They ended up raising him. He said he had a good life.

At last I was able to tearfully hug and thank Mildred Greene. I told her that to me she was and is an angel on earth. She told me that she was in the wrong place at the right time. Being a nurse, she knew she had to go to work helping the injured. I thanked her for doing what she could for Mom and Dad to stop their bleeding. She said that even though my Mom was injured, her only thoughts were of her children. Mildred told me that she wished the outcome would have been better for our family.

Mildred Tootie Green, the nurse who cared for Mom and Dad.

In closing I will say that the misery and confusion of that night was relieved by many acts of kindness and mutual assistance by many wonderful women and men. Without their help that night we would have lost hope and possibly perished as others did. We are so thankful for the aid our parents received from people who stepped forward to help. They made a difference.

Made in the USA
Columbia, SC
04 October 2021

46291841R00033